Central Scotland's Last Days of Steam

W.A.C. Smith

C000227041

When photographed on 5 May 1956, class V2 2-6-2 No. 60964, 'The Durham Light Infantry', was arriving at Polmont with the 6.00 p.m. from Edinburgh Waverley to Glasgow Queen Street, while class 4MT 2-6-0 No. 43141 was at the bay platform with the very last train for Bo'ness at 6.50 p.m. prior to withdrawal of the branch passenger service.

Text and photography © W.A.C. Smith
First published in the United Kingdom, 2006
Stenlake Publishing Ltd.
54-58 Mill Square, Catrine, KA5 6RD
www.stenlake.co.uk
Printed by P2D, 17 Burgess Road, Hastings, TN35 4NR

ISBN 9781840333664
The publishers regret they can not supply copies of any pictures featured in this book.

On a very wet 10 September 1955 class 4MT 2-6-0 No. 43141 was leaving Polmont with the 2.43 p.m. to Grangemouth while class J36 0-6-0 No. 65246 waited to reverse out to the locomotive depot. The mogul required to round the train at Falkirk Grahamston Station, opened in 1850 by the Stirlingshire Midland Junction Railway, to gain access to the Grangemouth branch, which had been opened in 1860 by the Forth & Clyde Canal Company.

Introduction

Stretching from Alloa and Stirling in the east to Balloch and Helensburgh in the west, the railways of Central Scotland were of immense interest, ranging, as they did, from the scenic delights of the Clyde coast and Loch Lomond, to main lines of the former Caledonian and North British Railways, busy suburban routes, the enormous Singer factory with its own station, a sprawl of collieries around Kilsyth and ironworks at Falkirk, a spectacular crossing of the River Forth, and a railway-owned port at Grangemouth.

There were also intriguing byways, now long gone, and which I first encountered in August 1945 on the occasion of a family outing to celebrate V.J. Day when we travelled from Glasgow Queen Street to Strathblane, hauled by class J39 0-6-0 No. 1504, and from there walked - by roads happily devoid of traffic thanks to petrol rationing - to Milngavie for class C16 4-4-2T No. 9444 which returned us to the city.

It has been said that little was done by the nationalised British Railways to popularise such lines - although I did travel to Aberfoyle in July 1949 with an evening excursion (at a fare of 3/6) which originated at Queen Street Low Level and consisted of eight elderly, gas-lit coaches in the charge of class J37 0-6-0 No. 64541. This may have been a delight for me, but for the ordinary passenger a service of two trains per day (three on Saturdays), which involved changing at Blanefield, the service's closure in 1951 - more than decade before the infamous Beeching cuts - came as no surprise.

What was a surprise, however, was that no one in authority seemed to recall that when, in the 1930s, the Big Four railway companies (LMS, LNER, GWR and SR) faced similar competition from road transport their reply was to slash fares and bring home to the public at large that the railways were alive and well by providing numerous excursion trains to coast and country and for special events large and small. Thus, to pick at random, a pre-war summer Saturday (3 June 1933) saw the LNER run thirty or more extra trains in Central Scotland, carrying an estimated 7,500 adults and 9,000 juveniles. These numbers were, of course, in addition to passengers travelling by scheduled services, and by LMS trains.

The 1955 Modernisation Plan sealed the fate of steam traction on British Railways, although final elimination did not take place until 1968 and steam to Helensburgh and Balloch had already ended in September 1961 and on the three-hour expresses between Glasgow and Aberdeen in September 1966. My own last journey behind a BR (as opposed to preserved) steam locomotive in Central Scotland was on Friday, 26 May 1967, when the Perth portion of the 1205 Euston to Glasgow (usually detached from the Glasgow train at Motherwell and worked to Perth by a diesel locomotive) was run as a separate train for the spring bank holiday weekend and was worked forward from Carlisle by Black Five No. 44795.

On 7 May 1960 Jubilee class 4-6-0 No. 45727, 'Inflexible', was photographed at Polmont with the 1.25 p.m. from Stirling to Edinburgh Princes Street. Black Fives and class 4MT 2-6-4Ts were the more usual motive power for these trains.

Acknowledgements

This volume is the thirteenth and last in the series. My thanks go to my partner Doris for her forbearance during the last six years the series has been in the making, and to my friend Tim Shuttleworth, also to Barry Hoper of the Transport Treasury for making prints from my negatives, and David Pettigrew of Stenlake Publishing for his editing.

Class C16 former North British Railway 4-4-2T No. 67495 awaiting departure from Grangemouth with the 3.10 p.m. train for Polmont on 22 January 1955. The passenger service, latterly operated by a diesel railbus, ended in 1968 and despite talk of reopening the branch to passengers this seems unlikely in view of the frequency of local bus services.

Black Five 4-6-0 No. 45319 leaving Grangemouth on 24 October 1964 with the 12.04 p.m. through train for Glasgow Buchanan Street, calling at Falkirk Grahamston, Falkirk Camelon, Greenhill and Cumbernauld. The dock lines at Grangemouth, seen on the right, were occasionally used by special passenger trains connecting with cruise ships.

Left Class 2P former Caledonian Railway 0-4-4T No. 55238 passing Fouldubs Junction with the 5.00 p.m. from Grangemouth to Polmont on 10 September 1955. A halt, named Thornbridge and mainly used by railway staff, was situated nearby, but had been closed in 1938. Fouldubs was junction for a goods line which avoided Falkirk Grahamston and was necessary in the days of heavy traffic from industrial establishments and Grangemouth docks.

Right Standard class 4MT 2-6-0 No. 76113 approaching Orchardhall on the Falkirk avoiding line with a freight train from Grangemouth, 12 September 1963. Part of this line remained in situ (as a single track) for many years after closure in 1968 awaiting an industrial development which never materialised.

Class J37 0-6-0 No. 64621 propelling a brake van across the swing bridge spanning the Forth & Clyde Canal at Orchardhall, 12 September 1963. Orchardhall was on the goods line from Grangemouth which bypassed Falkirk Grahamston Station.

The 2.35 p.m. from Polmont to Grangemouth was hauled by class C16 4-4-2T No. 67494 when photographed on 2 November 1957 at Falkirk Grahamston, where reversal was necessary. Eleven minutes were allowed for this manoeuvre, resulting in a schedule of 23 minutes for the six-mile journey.

Standard class 4MT 2-6-0 No. 76102 passing through Falkirk Grahamston Station on 13 February 1965 with an eastbound freight train. The station was rebuilt in 1986.

On 2 November 1957 the 2.16 p.m. from Grangemouth to Larbert was worked by former Caledonian Railway 0-4-4T No. 55204, seen here leaving Falkirk Grahamston.

Black Five 4-6-0 No. 45389 running into Falkirk Grahamston Station with the 1.26 p.m. train from Stirling to Edinburgh Waverley, 13 February 1965. The signal box was destroyed by fire in 1972.

Stirling Station, opened by the Scottish Central Railway in 1848, became an important traffic centre and was rebuilt in lavish style by the Caledonian Railway in 1914. On 16 July 1956 class D11 4-4-0 No. 62681, Captain Craigengelt, had arrived with the 1.08 p.m. train from Edinburgh Princes Street and class B1 4-6-0 No. 61076 headed the 3.05 p.m. departure for Alloa and Perth. 'Captain Craigengelt' (named after a character in a Sir Walter Scott novel) worked a train to Callander before returning to Edinburgh.

In the final years of steam traction on British Railways, Stirling provided a veritable parade of 'big yins'. Thus, on 5 June 1963, former LNER class A3 Pacific No. 60094, 'Colorado', was photographed arriving with 5.15 p.m. 'Granite City' three-hour express from Aberdeen to Glasgow Buchanan Street. The locomotive, built in 1928 and withdrawn from service in 1964, carried the name of the 1926 winner of the 2,000 Guineas.

In the evening sunshine of 31 August 1965 class A2 Pacific No. 60530, 'Sayajirao', departed from Stirling with the 6.15 p.m. from Glasgow Buchanan Street to Dundee. The locomotive's name commemorated that of a racehorse.

The 9.25 a.m. from Crewe to Perth ran daily (except Sundays) and was a popular train with enthusiasts both for travel and for photography as it remained steam hauled, with a variety of motive power, until April 1966. On 8 June 1963 I photographed class 6P 4-6-2 No. 72008, 'Clan Macleod', making a spirited departure from Stirling.

Coronation class 4-6-2 No. 46226, 'Duchess of Norfolk', at Stirling with a southbound train of parcels vans and empty stock, 8 June 1963. An LMS design dating from 1937, these magnificent machines were considered by many to be the finest steam locomotives ever built in Britain, but were condemned to a premature withdrawal in 1964 so as not to highlight the inadequacies of the diesels coming into service.

Class A2 Pacific No. 60527, 'Sun Chariot', made a brisk departure from Stirling on 8 June 1963 with the 1.30 p.m. 'Grampian' from Aberdeen to Glasgow Buchanan Street. Despite the disappearance of steam traction, the Stirling of today retains an impressive array of semaphore signals. 'Sun Chariot', the racehorse, was winner of the 1942 St Leger, Oaks and 1,000 Guineas.

Class B1 4-6-0 No. 61178 at Alloa with the 1.33 p.m. from Edinburgh Waverley to Stirling via Dunfermline, 17 June 1960. This service, which dated in part from 1852, ended in 1968. However, the section of line from Alloa to Stirling is currently being prepared for reopening, principally for the re-routing of freight trains from the Forth Bridge via Kincardine.

Preserved Caledonian Railway 4-2-2 No. 123, paired with its two restored Caley coaches, was photographed at Alloa on 3 October 1959, having conveyed members of the Edinburgh and Lothians Miniature Railway Club outward from Edinburgh Waverley over the Forth Bridge, return being via Larbert. No. 123, withdrawn in 1935, had been returned to service for special workings in 1958 at the age of seventy-two. It is now housed in the Glasgow Museum of Transport, while the coaches can occasionally be seen in service on the Bo'ness and Kinneil Railway.

Right The small locomotive shed at Alloa, opened by the North British Railway in 1885, was a sub-depot of Dunfermline MPD and housed some half dozen locomotives which found employment in shunting, local colliery traffic and (until closure) the Alloa branch passenger service. On 17 June 1960 I photographed class J38 0-6-0 No. 65903 at the shed which was closed early in 1967.

Left At Alva on 5 October 1953 driver Robertson and fireman Doyle welcomed me to the footplate of veteran class J36 0-6-0 No. 65307 (built by the North British Railway in 1899), which was heading the 3.48 p.m. branch train to Alloa. I was, in fact, the only passenger.

Class C15 former North British Railway 4-4-2T No. 67466 at Alva on 30 October 1954 with the last train for Alloa before withdrawal of the passenger service. This was due to leave at 1.28 p.m. but British Railways agreed to hold it back it until 1.33 p.m. to allow for my arrival from Glasgow.

In 1848 the Scottish Central Railway opened a branch from Alloa Junction, north on its main line north of Larbert, to South Alloa and in 1885 this was extended across the River Forth by a 1,600-feet-long, 20-span, swing bridge built by the Caledonian Railway. This brought the Caledonian to the port of Alloa, but the North British Railway had running powers over the line, and the preserved North British Railway 4-4-0 No. 256, 'Glen Douglas', was photographed crossing the bridge on 28 March 1964 with the 'Scottish Rambler' Easter railtour en route to Glasgow Buchanan Street. Services over the bridge finished in 1968 and now only the piers remain.

Class 7P rebuilt Royal Scot 4-6-0 No. 46160, 'Queen Victoria's Rifleman', passing the north signal box as it leaves Larbert with the 10.00 a.m. from London Euston to Perth, 31 July 1963.

Bonnybridge Canal, served by a short, steeply graded branch from Greenhill, was opened by the Caledonian Railway in 1886 and closed to passengers by the LMS in 1930. It was visited on 7 May 1960 by the Branch Line Society 'Scottish Central' railtour, which is seen here returning to the main line with its two preserved Caledonian Railway coaches hauled by Caley 4-4-0 No. 54465.

The Scottish Central Railway was opened from Greenhill to Larbert, Stirling and Perth in 1848. It was joined at Greenhill Lower by the Caledonian Railway from Carlisle and Glasgow and by a connection from the Edinburgh & Glasgow Railway at Greenhill Upper. On 18 September 1965 class J38 0-6-0 No. 65921 was photographed on the connection for Greenhill Upper Junction with a freight train from Alloa to Cadder Yard. Greenhill Station, on the former Caledonian route and seen on the left, was closed in 1967.

With the new town taking shape in the background, class V2 2-6-2 No. 60844 runs into Cumbernauld Station with the 10.00 a.m. from Dundee to Glasgow Buchanan Street on 18 September 1965. Cumbernauld has been served from Glasgow's Queen Street Station since closure of Buchanan Street Station in 1966. Its station was rebuilt in the 1980s.

Standard class 5MT 4-6-0 No. 73146 photographed passing Castlecary, one of the original stations on the Edinburgh & Glasgow Railway main line, with a westbound freight train on 28 May 1966. The station was closed the following year, but is remembered as the scene of several accidents, the worst of these occurring on 10 December 1937 in falling snow, when 35 passengers were killed in a rear-end collision between a down Edinburgh express, hauled by an A3 Pacific and a stationary train. On 2 September 1960, in patchy fog, an Intercity DMU ran into an up empty coaching stock train hauled by a tender-first Black Five. Nine of the DMU passengers were injured. On 9 September 1968 there was a collision and subsequent fire when a class 24 diesel locomotive embedded itself on the rear coach of a stationary Intercity DMU. The locomotive's two crew members were killed.

Situated between Castlecary and Croy, Dullatur Station was opened in 1876 and closed in 1967. Little trace remains of it today. On 15 July 1961 Black Five No. 45479 called with the 4.20 p.m. from Perth to Glasgow Queen Street (via the Devon Valley line) to pick up a bag of mail, and your photographer!

National Coal Board (Central West Area) 0-4-0 saddle tank No. 4, built in 1909 by the North British Locomotive Company of Glasgow, photographed crossing a swing bridge spanning the Forth & Clyde Canal with a loaded coal train on the former William Baird & Co. colliery system at Twechar, 13 June 1963.

Late on the evening of Friday, 26 July 1963, class B1 4-6-0s Nos. 61132 and 61330 were photographed approaching Lenzie with an ECS (empty coaching stock) train of thirteen vehicles from Cowlairs to Thornton Junction where they were to form relief services for the end of the Glasgow Fair fortnight the following day.

On 27 May 1957 passengers were photographed boarding the S.S. 'Sir Walter Scott' in spring sunshine at Stronachlachar for the 3.30 p.m. sailing along Loch Katrine to Trossachs Pier. The veteran steamer, built in 1900 by Denny of Dumbarton and assembled on the lochside, is now owned by the Steamship Sir Walter Scott Trust and continues to sail in summer.

Chartered trains traversing closed branch lines with vintage motive power, and known as railtours, proved popular with enthusiasts in the post-war years, but in 1952 the Chief Regional Officer for Scotland, a gentleman little known even to railway staff, apparently learned of their existence from a newspaper report and promptly banned such outings as dangerous! Fortunately, by 1958, he had been replaced by the charismatic James Ness as General Manager and not only did he go on to restore several historic locomotives to working order, but readily agreed to a resumption of railtours. As Area Secretary of the Stephenson Locomotive Society, I organised the first of these for 15 May 1958, covering the scenic Aberfoyle line (closed to passengers since 1951) and also including the Kilsyth branch. On a gloriously sunny day, veteran class J36 0-6-0 No. 65315 was well turned out by the shed staff at Eastfield and an unexpectedly large number of passengers resulted in the train loading to a maximum six coaches. With near punctual running throughout, the future of railtours in Scotland was assured! The train is seen here at the former Blanefield Station on the outward journey from Glasgow Queen Street.

Class K2 2-6-0 No. 61788, 'Loch Rannoch', at Balfron Station on the Aberfoyle line on 16 May 1959. It was hauling a special train, advertised as a 'Pioneer Railway Trip', which formed part of a Glasgow University extramural course on the History of Railways. The Edinburgh & Glasgow Railway had opened its Campsie branch from Lenzie through Kirkintilloch to Lennoxtown in 1858 and this was extended by small companies to reach Aberfoyle in 1882.

Steam dredger 'Clydeforth' photographed on 2 January 1958 during construction of a pedestrian underpass at Westerton on the Forth & Clyde Canal. 'Clydeforth' had been built in 1926 by the Grangemouth Dockyard Company for the LMS Railway (the Caledonian Railway having acquired the canal undertaking in 1867). Opened in 1790, and closed at the end of 1962, the canal was reopened to navigation in 2001.

Electric services on the Glasgow North lines commenced on 5 November 1960, but the Blue Trains were to be temporarily withdrawn on 18 December, following a series of electrical faults, and a steam service was substituted. This was no mean feat, and was overseen personally by James Ness, the energetic Scottish Region General Manager, as the locomotives and coaching stock previously used had been dispersed and in the event several locomotives were borrowed from the London Midland Region. These included class 4MT 2-6-4T No. 42426 which, on 28 August 1961, I photographed at Hillfoot Station, on the Milngavie branch, with an Airdrie-bound train. The Blue Trains resumed on 1 October and the branch, opened in 1863, is now partly single tracked.

In 1883 the Singer Manufacturing Company of New Jersey opened a factory at Clydebank for the manufacture of sewing machines and this eventually covered 110 acres, making it the largest single industrial complex in Scotland. It was served by Kilbowie Station (renamed Singer) on the former Glasgow, Dumbarton & Helensburgh Railway and by a terminal, with six platforms for the workers trains, which I photographed on 23 June 1961 with J37 0-6-0 No. 64633 and standard class 4MT 2-6-0 No. 76114, flanked by class V1 No. 67622 and class V3 2-6-2T No. 67621, heading departures for Springburn and Bridgeton. Singer Station is now served by the Glasgow North electric trains, but the worker's station closed in 1967 and its site, together with that of the factory, is now occupied by industrial units and a shopping centre.

Well turned out Black Five 4-6-0s Nos. 45118 and 45481 (from Carlisle Kingmoor Depot) at Kilbowie Station, on the erstwhile Lanarkshire & Dunbartonshire Railway and forming part of the Glasgow Central low level system, with the Royal Train, which was being serviced for a 3.30 p.m. departure from Clydebank Riverside Station for Windsor on 16 April 1953. It was conveying Her Majesty the Queen following the launch of the royal yacht 'Britannia' from John Brown's shipyard.

It was the end of the line for class 3P former Caledonian Railway 4-4-0 No. 54503 and class D11 4-4-0 No. 62675, 'Colonel Gardiner', as I photographed them awaiting cutting up in Arnott, Young's scrapyard at Old Kilpatrick on 14 January 1960.

For the Glasgow North electrification a connection was put in at Dunglass, west of Bowling and where the Caledonian line crossed the North British route, to allow trains from the latter to serve Dumbarton East Station. The diversion also had the advantage of eliminating a stretch of line at Dumbuck which was prone to flooding. On 9 April 1960 class V3 2-6-2T No. 67650 was photographed on this soon to be abandoned section while passing under the Caley line with the 12.14 p.m. from Balloch Central to Glasgow Queen Street Low Level, from where this train continued - by way of Springburn and Maryhill - to Milngavie.

Class K2 2-6-0 No. 61789, 'Loch Laidon', photographed at Dumbarton Central Station with the 3.00 p.m. summer Saturdays service from Glasgow Queen Street to Crianlarich Upper on 11 July 1959.

Standard class 4MT 2-6-0 No. 76004 joining the Helensburgh line at Dalreoch Junction with an *Orange Walk* special returning from Balloch to Glasgow on 11 July 1959. Note the industrial surroundings, which are unlikely to be seen at many lineside locations today with heavy industry in Scotland fast becoming a thing of the past.

Class 3F former Caledonian Railway 0-6-0 No. 57631 arriving at Alexandria with the 4.15 p.m. from Rutherglen to Balloch Central on 21 April 1956. This station, on the former Dumbarton & Balloch Joint Railway, had offset platforms. The branch, electrified since 1960, is now single track.

Left Balloch Pier Station, photographed on 26 June 1954 with class V1 2-6-2T No. 67628 on the 8.55 p.m. to Glasgow Queen Street Low Level and class 3MT 2-6-2T No. 40152 on the 9.05 p.m. to Glasgow Central Low Level. The trains connected with the veteran paddle steamer 'Prince Edward' on the 6.30 p.m. sailing from Ardlui at the head of Loch Lomond and with the 1953-built paddle steamer 'Maid of the Loch' which had given an evening cruise from Balloch.

Right Former Caledonian Railway 4-4-0 No. 54457 at Balloch Central with the 12.26 p.m. to Rutherglen on 7 April 1953. This station was replaced in 1988 by a platform on the east side of the roadway to facilitate removal of a level crossing. The half-mile extension to Balloch Pier Station had closed in 1981 upon withdrawal of the Loch Lomond steamer sailings.

Class K2 2-6-0 No. 61772 'Loch Lochy', at Balloch Pier with the 6.40 p.m. train for Bridgeton Central on 27 May 1957. It was conveying passengers off the P.S. 'Maid of the Loch' which can be seen on the left.

Above P.S. 'Princess May' at Balloch Pier for a 6.45 p.m. evening cruise on 30 August 1952. The Loch Lomond steamers were operated from 1896 by the Dumbarton & Balloch Joint Line Committee, representing the interests of the Caledonian and North British Railway companies (becoming, respectively, the LMS and the LNER from 1923 until nationalisation in 1948). 'Princess May', built in 1898 by A. & J. Inglis Ltd of Glasgow, was scrapped in 1953, by which time her attractive colours of grey hull and red funnel had been replaced by British Railways' drab black hull and yellow funnel.

Below P.S. 'Prince Edward' at Balloch Pier on 18 July 1953 after arriving with the 4.35 p.m. sailing from Ardlui. Launched in 1911 by A. & J. Inglis Ltd, 'Prince Edward' did not enter service on the loch until 1912, having missed the spring tide for getting up the river from Dumbarton. After sailing for two seasons in company with the new 'Maid of the Loch', which had been assembled on the lochside, the 'Prince Edward' was broken up in 1955.

Craigendoran Junction, photographed on the evening of 1 June 1957 with class V1 2-6-2T No. 67614 passing with the 6.06 p.m. train from Helensburgh Central to Bridgeton Central and class C15 4-4-2T No. 67460 coming off the West Highland line with the 5.17 p.m. push/pull from Arrochar and Tarbert. The LNER had introduced push/pull working on this service in 1940, the two-coach train being pushed from Craigendoran and pulled from Arrochar, and this was continued by British Railways until 1960 when a diesel railbus took over.

Class B1 4-6-0 No. 61358 at Craigendoran with the Sunday 7.18 p.m. to Edinburgh Waverley on 10 July 1955. The train had been reversed into the down (westbound) platform so that passengers coming off the paddle steamer 'Waverley' from a cruise did not have to trek over the station footbridge to join their train at the up (eastbound) platform. The pier platform, seen on the left and normally used for steamer connections, had been occupied by a train for Glasgow. Such consideration for customers is, of course, a long-forgotten aspect of our railways.

Built by A. & J. Inglis Ltd for the LNER in 1946, and replacing an earlier vessel of the same name lost during the Second World War, the paddle steamer 'Waverley' is seen approaching Craigendoran on 10 July 1953 on the 7.00 p.m. run from Rothesay. Craigendoran Pier ceased to be used for Clyde coast sailings in 1972. In 1974 Waverley was sold by Caledonian MacBrayne to the Paddle Steamer Preservation Society for a token £1. Now operated by the Waverley Steam Navigation Company, 'Waverley' continues to sail on the Clyde (and elsewhere) in summer.